1 The protection of non-designated heritage assets through local heritage lists

T0385713

1. Introduction

1 This Historic England Advice Note provides information on local heritage listing of heritage assets such as buildings, monuments, sites, places, areas or parks, gardens and other designed landscapes, to assist community groups, owners, applicants, local authorities, planning and other consultants, and other interested parties in implementing historic environment legislation, the policy in the National Planning Policy Framework (NPPF) and the related guidance given in the Planning Practice Guidance (PPG). This advice should be read in conjunction with other relevant Good Practice Advice and Historic England Advice Notes. Alternative approaches may be equally acceptable, provided they are demonstrably compliant with legislation and national policy objectives.

Definitions

The NPPF defines a heritage asset as a building, monument, site, place, area or landscape identified as having a degree of significance meriting consideration in planning decisions, because of its heritage interest.

Heritage assets are of two types: 'designated heritage assets', and 'non-designated heritage assets'.

Designated heritage assets are largely designated nationally under the relevant legislation (listed buildings, scheduled monuments, registered historic parks and gardens and registered battlefields), but also include world heritage sites, which are designated by UNESCO, and conservation areas, which are designated locally under relevant legislation. Designated heritage assets, with the exception of conservation areas and World Heritage Sites, are listed in the National Heritage List for England (NHLE), the official and up-to-date database of all nationally-protected historic buildings and sites in

England. Information about the different designation regimes and how to search the list can be found in the listing pages of the Historic England website. Designated heritage assets receive a greater degree of protection within the planning system than non-designated heritage assets; works to some assets, such as listed buildings and scheduled monuments, are subject to additional consent regimes. Information on conservation areas can be found on local planning authority websites.

Non-designated heritage assets are locally-identified 'buildings, monuments, sites, places, areas or landscapes identified by plan-making bodies as having a degree of heritage significance meriting consideration in planning decisions but which do not meet the criteria for designated heritage assets' (PPG). It is important to note that some non-designated heritage assets are equivalent to designated heritage assets in terms of significance – see text box following paragraph 27 below.

Non-designated heritage assets can be identified in a number of ways, including:

- Local heritage lists

- Local and Neighbourhood Plans

- Conservation area appraisals and reviews

- Decision-making on planning applications

2   This advice focuses on the production and review of local heritage lists but it will also help in the general identification of non-designated heritage assets. The preparation of local heritage lists is a way for communities, neighbourhood plan-making bodies and local planning authorities to identify and celebrate the historic buildings, places and spaces, archaeological sites and historic parks, gardens and other designed landscapes which enrich and enliven their area.

3   Inclusion on a local heritage list based on sound evidence and criteria delivers a consistent and accountable way of recognising non-designated heritage assets, no matter how they are identified, to the benefit of good planning for the area and of owners, developers and others wishing to understand local context fully. The process of preparing a local heritage list allows communities and neighbourhood plan-making bodies, in partnership with local planning authorities, to identify local heritage that they would like recognised and protected.

4   By providing clear and up-to-date information, backed by the policy in the National Planning Policy Framework, a local heritage list which has been made available on the website of the local planning authority (LPA) and via the Historic Environment Record provides clarity on the location of non-

designated heritage assets and what it is about them that is significant. Decisions are best made on the basis of published criteria, publicly available, so that clarity and certainty on their location and significance is available for communities, developers and decision-makers, therefore ensuring that they are given due consideration when change is proposed.

5   This advice draws on good practice across the country in developing a new local heritage list or making improvements to an existing one. Importantly, this advice should be seen as a starting point in the management of local heritage. In order to remain flexible enough to respond to local needs, decisions on the ways in which assets are identified, and the system adopted for managing the local heritage list, are matters for local planning authorities and their communities, including neighbourhood planning bodies in their area.

2.   Local heritage listing in the planning system

6   Protection of buildings and sites through local heritage listing relies on the planning system. It is therefore very important that the planning context is understood, as set out in the NPPF (Chapter 16: Conserving and enhancing the historic environment) and in the PPG. The NPPF (paragraph 185) advises that plans should set out 'a positive strategy for the conservation and enjoyment of the historic environment'. Emphasis is placed on 'sustaining and enhancing the significance of heritage assets' and recognising that heritage assets are an 'irreplaceable resource' which should be conserved 'in a manner appropriate to their significance' (paragraph 184).

7   Paragraphs 189-192 of the NPPF outline the matters which must be taken into account where proposals affect heritage assets. Paragraphs 189 and 190 give detail on the process which applicants and local planning authorities should follow in developing proposals and making and deciding applications concerning heritage assets, and paragraph 192 explains what local planning authorities should take into account in determining applications.

8   Whilst the planning protections for non-designated heritage assets are not as strong as those for designated heritage assets, they are still important. Specifically, paragraph 197 of the NPPF states that 'the effect of an application on the significance of a non-designated heritage asset should be taken into account in determining the application. In weighing applications that directly or indirectly affect non-designated heritage assets, a balanced judgement will be required, having regard to the scale of any harm or loss and the significance of the heritage asset'.

9   The Historic Environment section of the Planning Practice Guidance gives further information on non-designated heritage assets (paragraphs: 039-041). In particular it underlines the need for 'decisions to identify them as non-

designated heritage assets … [to be] based on sound evidence' and for 'all non-designated heritage assets [to be] clearly identified as such'; inclusion on a local heritage list is helpful (paragraph 040).

Significance and heritage assets

10   Significance, referred to above, is a guiding principle of heritage-related planning policy, of relevance to all forms of heritage asset across the continuum of designated to non-designated. The NPPF defines it as 'the value of a heritage asset to this and future generations because of its heritage interest. The interest may be archaeological, architectural, artistic or historic'. It may derive 'not only from a heritage asset's physical presence, but also from its setting'. Conservation is the process of maintaining and managing change to heritage assets in a way that sustains and, where appropriate, enhances their significance.

11   Heritage interests as defined in the PPG can inform the development of the criteria which are important in providing a sound basis for a local heritage list (see Part 2, Section 2, below):

- Archaeological interest: 'There will be archaeological interest in a heritage asset if it holds, or potentially holds, evidence of past human activity worthy of expert investigation at some point.'

- Architectural and artistic interest: 'These are interests in the design and general aesthetics of a place. They can arise from conscious design or fortuitously from the way the heritage asset has evolved. More specifically, architectural interest is an interest in the art or science of the design, construction, craftsmanship and decoration of buildings and structures of all types. Artistic interest is an interest in other human creative skill, like sculpture.'

- Historic interest: 'An interest in past lives and events (including pre-historic). Heritage assets can illustrate or be associated with them. Heritage assets with historic interest not only provide a material record of our nation's history but can also provide meaning for communities derived from their collective experience of a place and can symbolise wider values such as faith and cultural identity.'

12   Historic England Advice Note 12: Statements of Heritage Significance gives further information on the assessment of significance in applications for planning permission. The more information that can be provided about the significance of the asset and the reasons for its inclusion on the local list, the more effective its identification as a locally listed heritage asset will be.

Protection of non-designated heritage assets

13   The English planning system is plan-led. Where a local heritage list exists, it is therefore good practice to have a relevant policy in the Local Plan (and/or Neighbourhood Plan) which sets out how proposals affecting the non-designated heritage assets on the list will be considered.

14   In determining applications for planning permission that affect a non-designated heritage asset or its setting, the NPPF requires, amongst other things, both that local planning authorities should take into account the desirability of sustaining and enhancing the significance of such heritage assets, and of putting them to viable uses consistent with their conservation, and the consideration of the positive contribution that conserving such heritage assets can make to sustainable communities including their economic vitality (NPPF paragraphs 185 and 192).

15   These NPPF requirements mean that the conservation of a building or site on a local heritage list as a heritage asset is an objective of the NPPF and a material consideration when determining the outcome of a planning application (NPPF, paragraphs 8 and 184). Planning applications can be refused on the grounds of harm to a non-designated heritage asset. Local planning authority decision-making concerning non-designated heritage assets will benefit in clarity and transparency from the preparation and publication of a local heritage list.

16   Identification as a non-designated heritage asset may also demonstrate that a building or other heritage asset, such as a park or garden, makes a positive contribution to the character of a conservation area. Non-designated heritage assets within conservation areas also benefit from the general control over demolition in conservation areas afforded by the Town and Country Planning Act 1990.

17   The legitimacy and weight within the planning system of local heritage lists is increased when the list has been prepared in accordance with defined selection criteria, and has been subject to public consultation.

18   Planning permission is needed for works which constitute development. However, some works can be carried out without the need for planning permission, if they comply with Permitted Development Right provisions. Where a local planning authority is concerned that such changes may be detrimental to a heritage asset, they could consider the use of an Article 4 Direction to control them. Further information on Article 4 Directions and their use may be found in paragraph 53 of the NPPF, paragraphs 036 and 046 of the PPG, and Historic England Advice Note 1: Conservation Area Designation, Appraisal and Management.

3. Identification of non-designated heritage assets

19 Non-designated heritage assets can be identified in a number of ways, addressed in turn below:

- Local heritage lists (addressed in Part 2 of this advice)

- Local Plans

- Neighbourhood Plans

- Conservation area appraisal and review

- Decision-making on planning applications

20 In all cases, communities, neighbourhood forums, town or parish councils, and other community organisations may play a valuable role in the identification of non-designated heritage assets, and the development of relevant policy, as well as the local heritage lists themselves. Local heritage and amenity groups are likely to have a particular involvement, their experience and knowledge of the local area and its heritage being very helpful in the identification of non-designated heritage assets. However, just as lists developed by local authorities or neighbourhood forums are best progressed with the close involvement of the community, so those same groups should work closely with local planning authorities and neighbourhood forums, so that non-designated heritage assets are properly recognised, and considered appropriately within the planning system.

Local Plans

21 Local planning authorities have to make a Local Plan, setting out planning policies which will guide planning decisions in their area, including those covering heritage assets. Local plans have to be consistent with planning law and national policy and guidance and are expected to set out a positive and clear strategy for the 'pattern, scale and quality of development' including 'conservation and enhancement of the natural, built and historic environment, including landscapes and green infrastructure' (NPPF, paragraph 20, expanded on for the historic environment in paragraph 185). In developing this strategy, local planning authorities may identify non-designated heritage assets.

22 A local heritage list developed as part of the Local Plan process can become part of the Local Plan itself but this will introduce inflexibility: it will then only be possible to amend it as part of the Local Plan. Similarly, there is no need to include a local heritage list in a Supplementary Planning Document (documents which add further detail to the policies in the development plan), though this remains an option. It is however good practice for the Local Plan to contain appropriate policies to support protection of non-

designated heritage assets, wherever identified, as indicated in paragraph 13 above, and to provide clarity as to how a local heritage list will be used to inform decision-making.

Neighbourhood Plans

23   As outlined in Historic England Advice Note 11: Neighbourhood Planning and the Historic Environment, Neighbourhood Plans may establish policies for the development and use of land in a neighbourhood, thus becoming part of the development plan for the area. Work in preparing a Neighbourhood Plan may thus usefully include the development of a policy which sets out how proposals affecting non-designated heritage assets on a list will be considered, and consideration of which buildings and sites might merit inclusion on a local heritage list. The Historic Environment section of the PPG points out the usefulness of 'any designated and non-designated heritage assets within the plan area [being] clearly identified at the start of the plan-making process so they can be appropriately taken into account' (paragraph 005). A local heritage list prepared as part of a Neighbourhood Plan for an area will be produced through the community because these plans are researched, written and voted on by the people who live in the neighbourhood. They thus have direct power to develop a shared vision for their neighbourhood and shape the development and growth of their local area.

Conservation Area appraisal and review

24   Conservation areas are designated by local planning authorities (and some other bodies) to recognise an area of special architectural or historic interest. They are generally valued by those living and working in them as special places. Conservation areas may often contain buildings, archaeological areas or historic parks, gardens and other designed landscapes which are of local interest.

25   Conservation area appraisals may be a useful starting point for the identification of buildings, monuments, sites, places, areas or landscapes as non-designated heritage assets. One particularly relevant aspect of the appraisal process is the identification of unlisted buildings that make a 'positive contribution' to the character of a conservation area. More information about this can be found in Historic England Advice Note 1: Conservation Area Appraisal, Designation and Management.

26   The demolition of buildings in conservation areas requires planning permission, providing an additional degree of protection.

Decision-making on planning applications

27   Non-designated heritage assets may also be identified by the local planning authority during the decision-making process on planning applications, as evidence emerges. Any such decisions to identify non-designated heritage

assets need to be made in a way that is consistent with the identification of non-designated heritage assets for inclusion in a local heritage list, properly recorded, and made publicly available, for instance through an addition to a local heritage list, and through recording in the Historic Environment Record (HER).

Local heritage lists and archaeology

The majority of archaeological sites and landscapes remain undesignated. Scheduling is at the discretion of the Secretary of State, who may decide that it is not appropriate, even for sites which are found to be of national importance. Some archaeological sites cannot be designated because they are outside the scope of the Ancient Monuments and Archaeological Areas Act 1979 due to their physical nature, such as lithic scatters; these may be included in a local heritage list. Even in cases where they are added to a local heritage list, the interest and significance of archaeological assets may therefore also be national or regional. Clarity as to where there is potential for the discovery of such archaeological heritage assets is helped if plans, both local and neighbourhood, indicate areas where such potential exists; these can be noted in the Historic Environment Record.

The production of a local heritage list (or other process to identify non-designated heritage assets) can be a tool to identify and highlight both locally and nationally important, but unscheduled, archaeological sites, helping them to be given the appropriate level of consideration in planning decisions. Footnote 63 of the NPPF requires non-designated heritage assets of archaeological interest, which are demonstrably of equivalent significance to scheduled monuments, to be considered subject to the policies for designated heritage assets.

4. Further Information

28   Civic Voice, the national charity for the civic movement in England, has also published advice on local heritage listing as well as a register of local heritage lists.

2 Preparing and maintaining a local heritage list

Introduction

29 This section outlines the seven key stages in the production of a local heritage list, once the decision has been taken to create, review or revise one. As no single approach can be expected to apply to all areas, this approach can of course be individually tailored to take account of local circumstances.

Figure: Key stages in the development of a local heritage list

1. Commencement
Initiating a local heritage list

2. Criteria
Defining the scope of the local heritage list

3. Identification
Determining potential assets for the local heritage list

4. Assessment
Evaluating suitability of assets for the local heritage list

5. Approval
Finalising and confirming the contents of the local heritage list

6. Publication
Ensuring public access to the local heritage list, including through the Historic Environment Record

7. Review
Periodic review, revision and updating of the local heritage lists

1. Commencement - initiating a local heritage list

30 The context for developing a local heritage list will generally have been settled before work on the list begins. For example, whether or not the list will be part of the Neighbourhood Plan. This decision will also determine which body is responsible for its development. If it is to be developed within the community, then the body or bodies taking it forward would need to ensure that the programme is understood and that the local planning authority is part of the discussions.

31 When preparing a new local heritage list, or updating an existing one, public meetings, exhibitions and web-launches can be effective forums for bringing together interested partners before the process of identifying heritage assets begins. Starting a local heritage list in this way will develop awareness and encourage community involvement; it will also help to ensure that the process remains transparent. Where a local heritage list is developed as part of a Neighbourhood Plan, this community outreach will already be in train.

The value of working in partnership

32 Local heritage lists built on a strong partnership between the community and local authorities, including town and parish councils, are more likely to reflect the breadth of opinion on the historic environment in an area. A well-considered promotion and outreach campaign, working across both heritage and community teams at local authority level, and in partnership with leaders of diverse local community organisations, charities and heritage groups, is the best way of ensuring that local lists are inclusive and representative of the communities that surround them. Town and parish councils can also play a vital part in helping to establish and eventually formalise the list. The community has an important role in supporting the overall process, especially the development of selection criteria and the nomination of assets. Many government, non-government and commercial organisations also have an interest in, and maintain records on, potentially suitable assets and may be able to add to local knowledge if included in the process. Local Historic Environment Records (HERs), and the Historic England Archive will be particularly helpful sources of information.

33 The management of any non-designated heritage asset on a local heritage list will also be easier if it is included on the list with the knowledge of the owner. Owners should be advised of the intention to locally list an asset, including an explanation of the planning implications, but it is important to put in place a process for handling requests not to designate. Local heritage listing is a good opportunity to develop a dialogue with owners and to provide them with information on the significance of their property.

34 Local heritage lists should be inclusive in terms of the diverse social and cultural histories of many areas; therefore all parts of the community should be encouraged to participate, to ensure that a wide range of voices and histories is reflected in the local heritage list.

2. Criteria - defining the scope of the local heritage list

35 The table below gives commonly applied selection criteria for assessing the suitability of assets for inclusion in a local heritage list. Such criteria are often adapted from those used for national designations but it is important that the community develops criteria which respond to the local heritage of their area. These criteria are therefore given here as a suggestion of the kind of matters which those leading the development of a local heritage list may wish to consider, with further suggestions below.

36 The development of publicly accessible criteria will be very important for supporting the soundness of the list and the inclusion of heritage assets in it.

Criterion	Description
Asset type	Although local heritage lists have long been developed successfully for buildings, all heritage asset types, including monuments, sites, places, areas, parks, gardens and designed landscapes may be considered for inclusion.
Age	The age of an asset may be an important criterion, and the age range can be adjusted to take into account distinctive local characteristics or building traditions.
Rarity	Appropriate for all assets, as judged against local characteristics.
Architectural and Artistic Interest	The intrinsic design and aesthetic value of an asset relating to local and/or national styles, materials, construction and craft techniques, or any other distinctive characteristics.
Group Value	Groupings of assets with a clear visual design or historic relationship.
Archaeological Interest	The local heritage asset may provide evidence about past human activity in the locality, which may be in the form of buried remains, but may also be revealed in the structure of buildings or in a designed landscape, for instance. Heritage assets with archaeological interest are primary sources of evidence about the substance and evolution of places, and of the people and cultures that made them.
Historic Interest	A significant historical association of local or national note, including links to important local figures, may enhance the significance of a heritage asset. Blue Plaque and similar schemes may be relevant. Social and communal interest may be regarded as a sub-set of historic interest but has special value in local listing. As noted in the PPG: 'Heritage assets … can also provide meaning for communities derived from their collective experience of a place and can symbolise wider values such as faith and cultural identity'. It therefore relates to places perceived as a source of local identity, distinctiveness, social interaction and coherence, contributing to the 'collective memory' of a place.
Landmark Status	An asset with strong communal or historical associations, or because it has especially striking aesthetic value, may be singled out as a landmark within the local scene.

Table: Commonly applied selection criteria for assessing the suitability of assets for inclusion in a local heritage list

37   Local heritage listing can include all types of heritage assets, whether buildings, monuments, sites, places, areas or landscapes. Selection criteria are essential in defining the scope of the local heritage list and should take account of the range of assets in an area. This includes recognition that local distinctiveness may lie as much in the commonplace or everyday as it does in the rare and spectacular, subject to the asset in question having a degree of significance meriting consideration in planning decisions, because of its heritage interest. On the other hand, many locally important heritage assets reflect key aspects of nationally significant culture; designed landscapes, for instance, usually mirror national trends and these may equally merit consideration in planning decisions. Local heritage lists will be more valuable if supported by objective criteria, and if both criteria and content have been tested through public engagement.

Developing selection criteria

38   The national listing selection guides and supporting documents published by Historic England (dealing with listed buildings, scheduled monuments, registered parks and gardens, registered battlefields and protected wreck sites) set out further information on the types of criteria that can be adapted to local heritage listing.

39   Although criteria used for national designation can be readily adapted for local use, location-specific criteria may also be important in order to identify the heritage assets which are valued locally. The criteria for the selection of non-designated heritage assets, and the quality thresholds they should meet, should be made publicly available; good practice would suggest that they are included with the published list so that it is clear how the significance of the buildings and sites on the local heritage list have been judged, as well as information on their location (see also paragraph 58).

Wider context

40   The preparation of an overarching statement setting out local historic significance can be a useful aid to developing local selection criteria. This might take the form of a statement which succinctly identifies local characteristics – Historic England Advice Note 1: Conservation Area Appraisal, Designation and Management sets out a similar process for conservation areas. The preparation of such a statement is also a good opportunity to encourage wider community involvement. The statement could cover the following themes:

   ■   Cultural landscapes: heritage assets associated with a significant period in an area's history, including historic parks, gardens, grounds and their structures and other designed landscapes.

   ■   Social history: assets associated with the social and economic history of an area, including characteristic local industrial, commercial or agricultural activities; intangible aspects of heritage such as traditions and practices; or literary associations.

- Patterns of settlement: notable examples of planned or incidental planning including:

- Street plans;

  - Characteristic clusters of assets;

  - Interrelationship between buildings and open spaces;

  - Major and minor infrastructure, including the small-scale such as street furniture (for further information on the importance of streets and public spaces in the historic environment see Streets for All, published by Historic England).

  - Local Figures: assets associated with individuals of local importance including those identified by commemorative plaque schemes.

41   Historic England advice in support of Historic Area Assessments and other forms of characterisation also provides useful advice on assessing the nature and qualities of a defined area.

3.   Identification - determining potential assets for the local heritage list

42   A range of methods can be used to identify non-designated heritage assets, though no single method will produce a definitive local heritage list. Existing research publications are rich sources of information on potential local heritage list candidates. Public nomination is also a useful way in which to identify assets and has the added benefit of directly involving the community. The value and benefit to local communities of meaningful heritage participation is well-recognised, increasing heritage knowledge and skills and improving community wellbeing for example. Well-designed social media campaigns, and the use of digital mapping and polling platforms can significantly raise the profile and increase the reach of such campaigns beyond the usual communities and groups that participate in heritage. The local planning authority is likely to be central to determining what is included on the local heritage list though it may be compiled outside the local planning authority, by local neighbourhood plan-making bodies, amenity societies, Conservation Area Advisory Committees and/or local experts.

43   Regardless of the means by which candidate assets are identified, as a minimum, nominations need to be backed by information of sufficient detail and accuracy to demonstrate that they meet the requirements set by the selection criteria and by national planning policy.

A strategic approach

44   Before creating a new local heritage list, or reviewing an existing one, where a local heritage list is to cover an area wider than a Neighbourhood Plan area, it may be useful to take a strategic approach to its preparation. The approach taken in practice could be based upon any of the following methods:

- Plan-led: as part of the evidence-gathering for the Local Plan. See The Historic Environment in Local Plans (Historic Environment Good Practice Advice in Planning: 1) which stresses that 'Where the evidence base for the historic environment is weak, local planning authorities may need to commission proportionate research'. Heritage assets thus identified may be added to the local heritage list.

- Thematic: looking at the study area in terms of historic themes that are distinctive to the locality (for example industrial, military, high streets and designed landscapes).

- Asset type: similar to the thematic approach, but structuring the local heritage list based on asset type (for example buildings, and parks and gardens; although trees have their own system for protection, through Tree Preservation Orders, groups of trees may have their own historic significance, for instance orchards).

- Geographic: breaking down the study area into more manageable geographical units, for instance by parish, ward or neighbourhood; especially applicable to local authorities covering large areas or which are rich in heritage assets. Historic Landscape Characterisation is useful for understanding the local historic environment better; Historic England provides advice on the varieties of historic characterisation.

- Building on existing lists or sources of information: reviewing the old lists of 'Grade III' buildings (likely to be available in Historic Environment Records) or existing lists of significant conservation area, landmark buildings or parks and gardens.

Surveying existing sources of information

45   Individual HERs will be useful sources of information on non-designated heritage assets, as may local records offices and county archives. Publications and databases held by community, third sector and government and non-government organisations may similarly be potential sources. Assets considered, but rejected, for national designation may be good candidates for local heritage lists, provided they meet the local selection criteria – the Heritage Gateway is a useful resource for identifying such heritage assets. An assessment carried out for national designation, even if unsuccessful, will help in understanding the heritage asset.

46 The kind of material available in HERs is listed in Managing Significance in Decision-Taking in the Historic Environment (Historic Environment Good Practice Advice in Planning: 2). Local amenity societies and scholarly societies will have knowledge and possibly lists of locally significant heritage assets. Designed landscapes that have been identified in the Historic England Register Review are included in lists held by Historic England and by HERs; County Gardens Trusts are also a useful source of information, for instance through their research and recording activity. Historic Environment Advice Note 1: Conservation Area Appraisal, Designation and Management also contains useful information on survey and research in the local historic environment.

Public nomination

47 Public nomination can form a key element of the process. This will be helped if supported by a nomination form to guide those wishing to put forward a building or other heritage asset for consideration. It is also helpful if local planning authority officers provide advice to nominators on the type and amount of information required to support any application. The types of information that are likely to accompany nominations include:

- Location details: Ordnance Survey (OS) grid references and street address.

- Administrative information: may include Parish, District and County details.

- Local significance: identification of the significance of the asset in the local context.

- Photographs: visual recording of the asset from the public realm, concentrating on significant elements.

48 While the collation of supporting information would normally be undertaken by the nominator, the experience of local experts, voluntary organisations or local authority staff may also be a valuable addition.

4. Assessment - evaluating suitability of assets for the local heritage list

49 To qualify for local heritage listing nominated assets will need to meet the requirements of the selection criteria, and national planning policy. Assessment processes, including public consultation, are helpful in identifying errors or inaccuracies in supporting information.

50 It is also important to identify assets at the assessment stage that should not be added to the local heritage list, including buildings or sites already included as designated heritage assets in the National Heritage List for England, as these are already subject to other forms of protection and

duplication would be both unnecessary and unhelpful. Ensuring that the public has sufficient access to existing Information (such as through records on the local Historic Environment Record (HER), Heritage Gateway (a tool for cross-searching records including Historic England designation records), or related databases) will minimise the likelihood that assets already covered by national statutory designation will be nominated.

Selection panels

51   Selection panels can be an effective way in which to assess nominated assets independently. Membership could helpfully be drawn from a representative cross-section of the community and not restricted to professionals. The panel's primary responsibility will be the production of a shortlist that can be presented for public consultation.

Specialist knowledge

52   It may occasionally be necessary to seek specialist advice when assessing a particular asset type. The first source of expert knowledge will usually be from within the local authority, with external specialists supplementing this expertise where necessary. The voluntary sector often holds information and expertise of high quality, for instance County Gardens Trusts, county archaeological societies and local vernacular architecture and industrial archaeology groups.

Assets of potential national significance

53   Assets of potential national significance may be identified as part of the local heritage listing process. Such nominations should be referred to Historic England in the normal manner – further information on how to apply for designation can be found on Historic England's website. The proposal of an area-based asset or a group of assets may suggest that the area has particular special interest beyond local heritage interest; the local planning authority may then need to consider designating a new conservation area or extending an existing one.

Finalising the nomination shortlist

54   Before the group, neighbourhood plan-making body or local planning authority ratifies the final local heritage list, public comment can helpfully be sought. Comments received in response to the publication of the shortlist may be of additional use in confirming the suitability of adding an asset to the local heritage list.

55   Particular attention should be given to responses received from the owners of assets as these will assist in developing future management strategies. Although there is no statutory requirement to consult owners before adding an asset to the local list, inviting comment may provide information that is important for understanding its significance. The responsibility for assessing

any requests not to list could fall to the selection panel or local authority staff, but it is important that a procedure is put in place for handling requests from owners not to designate, and this procedure adequately publicised.

5. Approval - finalising and confirming the contents of the local heritage list

56   For local authority-compiled lists, once the assets on the shortlist for nomination have passed all the necessary checks, final endorsement can be sought at the appropriate level within the local planning authority, which might include Committee or Cabinet Member sign-off. Nevertheless, as a local list is unlikely to be considered definitive and further additions may be required during the course of planning decisions, local planning authorities should ensure that officers have the ability to assess heritage assets for inclusion within the local list and either the delegated authority to add them to the list, or to seek a rapid decision through a clearly-defined procedure.

57   Where a community group is creating the list, this will need to be signed off by the group itself prior to being adopted by the local authority concerned, in order for it to be given proper weight in planning decisions: formal ratification ensures public confidence and maximises the influence of the local heritage list as a material consideration. Where a Parish or Town Council or Neighbourhood Forum is preparing a local list for a Neighbourhood Plan, the LPA's agreement to the local list is not needed, but the LPA will be an important stakeholder at the examination stage, and will be the body responsible for deciding whether to accept the examiner's recommendations, whether to take the plan to referendum and, ultimately, whether it should be made. As such it is sensible to work closely with the local planning authority's heritage advisers, who will also be responsible for informing the council's decisions affecting the locally listed assets.

6. Publication - ensuring public access to the list, including through the Historic Environment Record

58   Publishing the finalised list is very important. To ensure that it protects non-designated heritage assets through the planning system, it needs to be published by the local planning authority, ideally electronically (for example, on the local planning authority's website). An illustrated local list is to be encouraged, for clarity regarding the assets identified, as well as interest, and it would also be useful to indicate in the published list the criteria under which heritage assets have been included (as indicated, for instance, in the List of Buildings of Townscape and Heritage Value appended to the Fleet (Hampshire) Neighbourhood Plan 2018-32). The local list of non-designated heritage assets in the Dorchester-on-Thames Neighbourhood Plan (Oxfordshire) tabulates the information clearly and provides useful background information. The local list for Sevenoaks (Kent) is map-based and, like the Fleet list, illustrated.

59   Linking the local heritage list to the local planning authority's geographic information system (GIS), as the Sevenoaks Local List is, will also guarantee that planning applications affecting locally listed assets can take full account of the significance the community attaches to those assets. This will further ensure local heritage lists are able to inform local planning authority decision-making.

Historic Environment Records and local heritage lists

60   Historic Environment Records can play a crucial role in ensuring access to the information supporting local heritage list preparation. The NPPF (paragraphs 187 to 189) emphasises the importance of HERs in providing the core of information needed for plan-making and individual planning decisions. HERs are unique repositories of information relating to landscapes, buildings, sites and artefacts. Their content underpins the identification, recording, protection and conservation of the local historic environment and the interpretation of historic environment designation and planning decisions. HER recording guidelines vary across the country. Individual HERs are best placed to advise on how to collect and collate supporting data.

61   The inclusion of a site or structure in an HER does not itself identify it as a non-designated heritage asset: inclusion merely records valuable information about it, and does not reflect the planning judgement needed to determine whether it does in fact have a degree of heritage significance which merits consideration in planning decisions. However, the information within the HER will help to identify candidates for possible inclusion in a local heritage list.

62   In addition to supporting local heritage list preparation, Historic Environment Records are also repositories for the lists themselves. To ensure that Historic Environment Records are kept up-to-date, and that local heritage lists are accessible, clear procedures are needed to support the swift addition of local heritage lists to the relevant HERs, as well as for any amendments which are subsequently made to the lists.

Publication on the local planning authority website

63   The local heritage list should be published on the local planning authority website, as well as being added to the Historic Environment Record. Accessibility and value to users is likely to be maximised by an innovative and imaginative approach to presentation, with direct links to data and maps where possible.

7. Review - periodic review, revision and updating of local heritage lists

64   Local heritage lists benefit from periodic review and revision. A review may include adding new buildings or sites or removing those that no longer fulfil the selection criteria. The review period is best decided at the local level but could be timed to coincide with the release of new information such as a new or updated conservation area appraisal and will, of course, be dependent upon resources. Reviews can also be made on an on-going basis (as and when nominations are received) or may be held once a set number of nominations have been submitted. Removal of assets from the list may be appropriate in circumstances where an asset no longer meets the criteria for selection, has been demolished, or has undergone changes that have negatively impacted its significance.

65   Local heritage lists are also likely to need updating between reviews, for example in response to the identification of non-designated heritage assets through the decision-making process for planning applications. Revising Local Plans, Neighbourhood Plans and conservation area appraisals can be a useful trigger to do so. A change in the criteria for designation on the list may also provoke a review. But even where there is no external prompt, it is still useful to revisit the list to check that heritage assets included still merit inclusion on the list and to check that heritage assets identified in the planning process have been added to the list, thereby maintaining a local heritage list's value and relevance.

66   As local heritage lists are therefore unlikely to be definitive, local planning authorities should ensure that there is a mechanism for additions to be made. This may be by officers having the ability to assess heritage assets for inclusion within the local list, and either the delegated authority to add them to the list or to seek a rapid decision through a clearly-defined procedure.

3 Further mechanisms to protect local heritage

67 Outside the planning system, there are other ways of safeguarding local heritage which is of importance to the local community. One such is the identification of Assets of Community Value.

68 The Localism Act 2011 requires local authorities to maintain a list of assets of community value (ACV) that have been nominated by the local community. If an asset is listed as an ACV, and comes up for sale, the community then has six months to put together a bid to buy it. There may be some overlap between ACVs and local heritage assets: as long as they meet the requirements set out in the Localism Act 2011, heritage assets on a local heritage list may also qualify as assets of community value.